"Malissa is a sister I could call on at anytime. Her words of wisdom and encouragement in any season have been a blessing. The anointing on her life is impactful."
-*Elena George, Emmy Award Winner, Celebrity Makeup Artist*

"My sister, my friend, my minister, Malissa Redmond! I love and appreciate her for her anointed ministry that is expressed in so many ways . . . music, prayer, spoken word, beautification artistry, and more! The foundation of it all is her servant's heart that is a tangible expression of God's love to any and all who encounter her. Thank you Malissa for 'singing over me' and shifting the atmosphere in my world."
-*Heather Hughes, Celebrity Stylist, StyleUnleashed*

"Minister Malissa Redmond is caring, compassionate, and truly a breath of fresh air in The Body of Christ. She has shown by example that although faced with many trials and tribulations, God has the final say! She is an inspiration to ALL she comes in contact with. Through her ministry, my life has forever changed for the better. She is an *overcomer*!"
-*Lisa S. Dozier-Annunziata, Lisa S. Dozier Funeral Services Inc.*

"Overcomer is *more* than appropriate when it comes to Malissa Redmond. Her anointing is second to none. Her presence is a testimony to the fight in her. Her voice is angelic and her words of wisdom are timely from Heaven. A true child of God."
-*DJ Tony Tone, Blessed Kept Secret (BKS)*

"Malissa Redmond is the epitome of an overcomer. I've witnessed the way she pours into everyone in her life, teaching them to speak the word over and through every situation. Her faith in God and knowledge of His word is something to behold."

-Nicholas Ryan Gant, Musician

"Malissa, where do I begin? She's a detailed strategist, team player, and woman of God! I had an opportunity to work with Malissa when I was in a vulnerable state—a moment in my life when I put my name on the line, and questioned if I had dreamed too big. A phone call at 12:30am turned into a year-long relationship, working and building together. I never thought one phone call would turn into a dialogue with Malissa almost every day, as it relates to business. We have talked business, prayed together, and kept our faith in the Lord. It has been a pleasure to see Malissa utilize her talents for the service of others, providing quality and memorable moments at events far and above people's expectations. I look forward to seeing what the Lord will do with her and her business, to serve others who are in need. Love always!"

-Phil Taitt, The Phil Taitt Show Host

"Malissa is a prolific worship leader and singer whose true gift is the reflection of Christ's likeness that she walks in. She's never been too busy to laugh, to smile, to listen, and to encourage someone. I'm proud to call her sister and friend."

-Brian Everett Francis, Photographer, BeePhaizon

Overcomer

Discover the Champion in You

Also by Splendor Publishing

Overcomer

Discover the Champion in You

MALISSA REDMOND

Splendor Publishing
College Station, TX

SPLENDOR PUBLISHING
Published by Splendor Publishing
College Station, TX.

First published printing, May, 2017.

Library of Congress Control Number: 2017939695
Overcomer: Discover the Champion in You

ISBN-10: 1-940278-22-8
ISBN-13: 978-1-940278-22-3
1. Self-help 2. Spirituality

Printed in the United States of America.

Cover Photo: Dreamstime, Milacroft, 7757619

Back Cover Photo:
Photographer, Sabrina Lamour
Makeup, Tambela Holmes
Hair, Michell Jenkins
Stylist, Malissa Redmond

For more information or to order bulk copies of this book for events, seminars, conferences, or training, please contact SplendorPublishing.com.

Dedication

To my grandmothers, Della Mae Joyner and Corine Smiley:
words cannot express the gratitude I have for the love given,
wisdom shared, and strength displayed.

To my beautiful cousin, Mecca Joyner-Ortiz:
I know you would've been proud. To my sister, Michelle
Gillyard: I watched you overcome battles to the very end.
I love and miss you both so much.

To my family: thank you for your endless prayers,
encouragement, and presence in my life.
I'm better today because of each of you.

Contents

"And they overcame him by the blood of the lamb and by the word of their testimony . . ."

Revelation 12:11 *KJV*

Foreword

Do you know why you have this book in your hands? It's because it's time for you to embrace your true identity through the testimony of this angel.

You are more than a conqueror.

You are God's chosen.

You are Christ's ambassador.

You are the temple of the Spirit.

And my sister's story will inspire you to look in the mirror, pray, declare, and believe that you too are an overcomer! Too many around us suffer in silence.

To paraphrase the great Maya Angelou, what happens to you in life can change you but it does not have to define you.

We can't be healed if we deny our wounds. And we can't be healed if we make our wounds into a shelter from life's storms. It is okay not to be okay. But it is not God's will to allow our spiritual pain and our spiritual enemy to define us.

Jabez was named in pain. But he cried out to God believing that there was yet more for his life and legacy! Minister Malissa Redmond's story is a modern day prayer of Jabez for women and men everywhere who need to know or be reminded that nothing is impossible with God!

Real life change, and the Spirit's available power, is not in the spectacular or the spooky. Christ's saving grace does not come in the sensational packages of many modern day religious speakers.

As you will read in the pages that follow, Christ will meet you, guiding your steps as a loving Father towards a prodigal teen. He will root you in a church you don't fully understand to reveal his holiness. Our Lord will open your eyes to see others through his eyes—even those who cause you pain. You will see the steady process of the Spirit not only healing the body, but liberating the soul. Jesus can meet you on the do-or-die streets of Brooklyn, NY or even while you read this book.

Psychotherapist and Holocaust survivor Viktor Frankl said, "Those who have a 'why' to live, can bear with almost any 'how'." We may not always know why we are suffering; but in Minister Redmond's story you can see clearly *who* was working in her both to will and to keep standing. And after learning to stand in faith, Minister Redmond understands a little bit more about "why" she has suffered setbacks and setups . . . for you! That's right. You are part of the reason, because you need this book right now. You are meant to overcome. Embrace the journey, the process, and The Lord Jesus Christ who came that you might have an abundant life.

Dr. Onorio Chaparro

Brooklyn, New York

Preface

Throughout the years, victories and defeats have been measured by individuals encountering obstacles seemingly too difficult to overcome. One's victory can be scaled by their success after a trial. Life itself has the capacity to challenge the strongest person, due to their lack of foresight, inability to control situations, and fear of failing or being rejected.

Often, when crisis comes, it exposes as well as signifies opportunities for growth and well-needed change. For reasons such as complacency, arrogance, and self-righteousness, a person can make the need for change obsolete. The danger in not changing when necessary is costly. Ask yourself: are you willing to pay the price? Who will be affected or infected as a result of your decision? Are stubbornness, fear, and pride justifiable? Must tragedy take place for you to adhere to change? What is this crisis telling you? Who are you becoming?

Some say experience is the best teacher; however, it is not based on truth. It is based solely on opinions. For example, it's not necessary to experience something in order to determine its effects. Through observation and facts you can see the direct result of drug usage, unprotected sex, poor decision making, and the list goes on.

Humanity craves what is forbidden. In the Garden of Eden, this craving was entertained, nursed, and exposed. Although the Creator, Elohim, gave clear instructions regarding what was forbidden and what benefits humankind could enjoy, the Adamic nature ultimately gave way to the fall that still affects humanity today (Genesis 2:15). Many believe that when you know better you do better, or that common sense is common, but we understand that is not fact nor is it truth. Society is filled with individuals who choose their way without regard to their pedigree, influence, responsibilities, or to the goals they have that were set by others and themselves. A room filled with people sharing ideas, does not guarantee understanding or revelation of the information shared. Does this make one more intelligent than the other? Absolutely not! No two people are alike, not even siblings who are multiples are totally identical, which tells us that God intended for us to all possess, appreciate, and responsibly display our uniqueness.

In the eighties, advertisements displayed messages like, "Crack Kills," "Aids Awareness," and other informative messages to increase consciousness of the existence of the negative and to also make people aware of the resources available as preventative methods. Simply put, cause and effect. Here is why parents and advocates teach adolescents to say "No" to drugs, abstain from sex, and refrain from reckless behavior and the like. The society we live in is often ruthless and prideful. A prideful people accompanied by arrogance and the need for independence, has been the driving force of generations. There's nothing new under the sun.

An African proverb states, "It takes a village to raise a child." It's true, yet this concept is not always in operation to reap the benefits of building healthy communities across the world. This proverb simply means, we're designed to cohabitate, co-labor, and cooperate—investing in one another as we build healthy communities and develop individually. It can be the difference in an individual or family doing well, excelling in school, and advancing in society. Often, we leave people to themselves and expect positive results. Are you yours brother's keeper? How involved are you in your village/community? To what degree will you reach out, beyond your comfort zone?

The power to choose is a gift! Be responsible with every choice. To not choose is still an intelligent choice! We have the option to learn from others and to partake, and to deal with the consequences whether good or bad. Knowledge is power and an incredible tool in the hands of the wise. It can also become a weapon.

What you don't know could be hurting you!

Acknowledgements

To my Heavenly Father, I give you thanks for being the common thread in my life; you've been consistent and reliable through every season. I'm grateful for every gift given for your glory. You chose me to steward many things and grace me to overcome any challenge because of your unfailing love.

To my husband, Red, Mr. Derrick Redmond, we started this journey together many years ago. You've loved me with flaws and all. Through the good and bad, you saw my brokenness, gifts, strengths, and weakness. You decided to commit to the process of love and you continue to cover me. Thank you for being you!

To our beautiful children, Davon, D'Asia, D'hane, and Dallas, you're God's greatest gifts to me. You've shared me with the world, the church, and even your friends who are now our family too. Your vantage point of the journey is significant and special. Thank you for your individuality and presence . . . Love, Mommy

Special thanks to my support systems: my parents, Lloyd and Joyce Smiley; my siblings, Steve, Vette, and J ("The Four Smileys") who are the inspiration for my business, ForSmiles Inc.; my extended family; my medical family; and my spiritual family, Rugged Cross Baptist Church and Christian Cultural Center. To my pastors Dr. A.R. and Pastor Karen Bernard, thank you for your presence, patience, support, and love for me and my family.

Chapter 1

The Blues

In life, seasons are not measured by the calendar year. Some are longer than others and diverse in experiences, with the overall objective being, "to grow through, not just go through." Maximizing potential in adverse circumstances can sometimes be an astronomical goal, especially to the faint of heart. It's inevitable for seasons to change. The process of change is significant, and there are indicators that determine the unique characteristics of each new season. What's true in the spiritual is also true in the natural.

In winter, the trees bare their souls while in the spring the flowers bring forth their beauty. Autumn's leaves vary in shape, color, and majesty, and summertime anywhere is radiant, vibrant, and alive. Life's calendar is not mirrored by the natural calendar; however, bearing fruit that remains is imperative in any season for successful living. Waking up to a clear blue sunny sky, listening to the crashing of the waves against the rocks, while birds sing sweet melodies in harmony is breathtaking! Take a breath . . . let it out. Enjoy the moment.

A gorgeous day like this is the most beautiful encounter and observation to someone who is free, clear in their thinking, and optimistic. Opening sleepy eyes to such glory in the morning is someone's dream vacation and another's reality, however, in the mind of someone exposed to negativity, even the most beautiful day could be a flashback from hell . . . a devastating experience. It's all about perspective.

"The blues" has the ability to dim your view, making beautiful days appear as potential bad days because history repeats itself. Someone say "Mindset!" Your mindset sets the tone, manages your expectations, and guides your goals. Well, my mindset was consistent, yet unchanged for the better. Excitement is in the air when summertime is just around the bend. The sounds of laughter, neighbors conversing, and music playing, reflect diversity in cultures that broaden barriers and boarders. The significance of cars riding by bumping the hottest jams, sub woofers setting off car alarms, and Mr. Softee's music from the ice cream truck indicates the season's change, awakening the kid in all of us. Can you feel the change in the air?

Allow me to give you a view of the blues from my point of view—just an excerpt, seen through a lens colored by a heart dimmed by the cares of this world . . . a heart too young to understand but very much aware of pertinent details. Just snap your fingers, pat your feet, and go with me on this cold, cold journey—a journey of a young, multitalented and resilient girl, discovering her value, and *determined* to not just coexist.

Some seasons are dark, grey, cloudy, dreary, dreadful, tiring, extremely exhausting, and dry. At any given time, things may be beyond your control; you may be subject to the terms and conditions presented on the outside, but you don't have to be internally damaged or paralyzed. Even in times like these you have the power to choose. It may take more effort to exude joy or even to be productive. Activity doesn't equate to productivity. The blues can be born in times like these. As a matter of fact, a genre of music was birthed from this very place. We call it, "The Blues." Singing the blues signified pain, hurt, abandonment, and loneliness, and the storytelling was a discovery of possible betrayal or sadness. Elvis Pressley began "Heartbreak Hotel" with a line like, "Since my baby left me!" It sounds as though he was having problems in the relationship area and needed to sing about it. As a writer/singer, I find it easier to sing about experiences and feelings rather than just talking about them to someone else. There's nothing like sweet harmonies over a melodic bed with lyrics speaking from the heart to the soul, snapping fingers. I remember the day I realized I had the blues. I didn't identify it as the blues at the time. Sadness flooded my heart as my life unraveled from the seams, losing the grip on my perception of family. Realizing I had people around but not really having someone "there" created roots that I'm still uprooting today. As a pre-teen, life should've been exciting as I was transitioning to junior high school, with no real responsibilities except doing well in school, attending church, and doing chores. You'd think everything was smooth sailing, but family life was far from good, economically, emotionally, mentally or even socially. We were on public assistance. Silence was loud, and food scarce. We grew up in the projects with stigmas placed on us because of it. We were the black sheep.

My heart was broken in pieces with feelings of despair, abandonment, and fear. Dad was in the Air Force and worked for TWA airlines so it was normal for him to be away. Even today he loves to travel! Traveling to various places for work and pleasure was his way of life. In fact, I don't remember waking up to him being in the house, him tucking us in at bed time, or anything indicating that he was staying or lived with us. Some things I've blocked out, and it will take some serious digging to pull them up. As a child the ball of confusion started as seeds and kept mounting with each disappointment. His word meant everything to me, even when I tried my best not to give it permission. Everything hinged on his love, approval, and acceptance. His word diminished in value with each broken promise. Something inside of me hoped, even still. Many days I'd sit on the radiator near the second-floor window in the hallway, expecting his car to pull up because he said he was coming . . . but he just didn't come, neither did he call to say things changed. As an adult, it bothers me if I make plans with someone or if someone gives me their word and with no consideration to communicate, their plans fall through. It especially bothers me when it's coming from an individual I trust, value, or consider close. Things happen, I understand, but disregarding commitments and poor communication reflect on a person's character. I've heard it said, "All you have is your word and your name." Your reputation precedes and follows you!

As a kid I understood through negative actions, what mere words could not repair, and it was detrimental to me.

What a fight it was to get my dad to keep his promises! This happened so many times with no apology, explanation, acknowledgement that I began building a wall to protect my heart, but my mind was left to wonder. This wall or force field also became my very own prison. Struggling mentally and emotionally became the daily routine. Daddy was the first male to break my heart. One day I went to the top of my six-story building and contemplated suicide. The roof was gated, the ground was filled with rocks, and the night sky was beautiful and clear. Tears blurred my vision with every blink as they were falling uncontrollably. With everything in me I screamed my frustrations into the air in hopes that God—whom I learned about in Sunday school, sang about in the choir, and told others about—would somehow hear me and take away this chronic anguish and pain. I didn't want to die physically; I just wanted the pain and sadness to stop! Confusion built with each day, moments seemed like months, sometimes years. As I climbed the gate without fear, something wouldn't just let me jump. I now believe that it was God. He didn't say anything: the clouds didn't roll back, I didn't see an angel, but there was an inner peace confirming that jumping wasn't the way out. Slowly my tears stopped, drying on my face. Then I came down off the roof with my mind and heart racing, and my secret suicide attempt. Although I had friends, a large family, and I was socially active, I wanted to feel real love and affection from my first male role model, whom I called, "Dad."

I wondered why a twelve-year old was on a roof at any time of the day, especially in her pajamas! In hindsight, it was mommy who had the real "blues." Though she was never clinically diagnosed, the symptoms, signs, and fruit were there. As I reflect back, my heart aches for her. Mommy would sit in front of the TV from sun up to sun down unless there was a prayer meeting, Bible study, or it was the weekend. She developed the art of tuning us out in her favorite chair, drowning in her own depression. Interestingly enough, she only seemed alive at church or with the Joyner family on weekends and holidays. Her quiet strength could easily have been mistaken for weakness because she was not much of a talker. Grandma Mae was her very best friend! They'd talk every day, even if it was for just a minute. I noticed the change in her when she became pregnant with my younger sister. My mom and I went pretty much everywhere together, with me being the baby for eleven years. I slept in her bed until I was about eight or nine years old, tucked securely right behind her. My first day of kindergarten seemed like the longest day ever because my buddy—mommy—wasn't there. Separation anxiety is real; it's scary and has to be overcome by love because perfect or mature love casts out fear. That love must first be discovered then accepted. I lived right across the street from my school, PS 273 (The Wortman School). Even though I was familiar with the outside of the building, it was a long, hard day inside those big doors without my best friend, my mommy.

The blues don't show up over night, they manifests over time. Unfortunately, unbroken cycles can perpetuate the blues. Broken promises, devaluing someone, or any form of abuse or uncertain conditions can become breeding grounds for cultivating the melancholy mindset. This can paralyze an individual; during a "wilderness experience" one can find it difficult to juggle emotions and make sense of life as they know it.

As the children of Israel wandered for forty years, they experienced "the wilderness" because of their parent's decisions, and we too, were partakers of our parent's wilderness.

Poverty-stricken, we sometimes wondered where the next meal was coming from when we had more month left than money. While dad maintained his career, owned property, and appeared to be successful, we were left to make due, so I've been told. There were many people who abused the system trying to live beyond their means but that wasn't our story. Above being embarrassed to go shopping with food stamps, recertification day at the office on Pine Street with the social worker was the worst! Not being able to have nice things or ever take a vacation together was depressing. Our vacation time was the Joyner/Johnson family reunion and somehow mommy would make sure we went. She would pinch, save, and use the family payment plan in order for us to go, however, dad never came. What is a family vacation without the whole family? Family—as we knew it—was without a male covering, provider, or nurturer in the home. Maybe he had the blues too. As a parent, I can't understand what could separate you from enjoying life with family, protecting and building relationships, except the stronghold called "the blues." The blues will swallow up your day, leave you feeling empty, cloud your view, waste your time, steal your life changing moments, invade your space, crowd your heart, and delay true peace. The choices you make have consequences, so consider the people who can and will be affected by them.

Selfishness can drive the moment but regret can stay for a lifetime.

Reflection

Have you ever had "the blues"? If so, what did you do to get through them? Do you know someone who has the blues? In what ways can you help?

Reflection Notes: _____

_____

_____

_____

_____

_____

_____

_____

_____

_____

_____

_____

_____

_____

_____

Chapter 2

Church Girl

Church:
a place of public worship,
a body of people who attend or belong to a particular local church.

The Bible is filled with information revealing the character, attributes, power, laws and most importantly the love of God. These truths are written for all to see, however, they are revealed by the Holy Spirit (the Spirit of truth) to whomever He chooses to reveal himself to. There are those who read the living word as a novel filled with great biblical stories about life's triumphs, defeats, successes, and failures. For me, the Bible is foundational in my service to God and others. I was raised in the historic Rugged Cross Baptist Church where the late Rev. Desha Moten was our pastor. I received my introduction to God from home-church life, fellowshipping with other believers. Growing where I was planted was foundational as a Baptist church girl. From Sunday school, visiting other churches, anniversaries, special events, rehearsals, and the Baptist conventions, you would think that everyone attending were true believers on their way to heaven with many crowns and problem free. Whew! The reality is that attending church services religiously does not equate to having a healthy, growing, personal relationship with Almighty God, or with people. Neither does it signify authentic servanthood of the faithful attendees. Although I knew a lot about God, it didn't compare to knowing Him for myself. He was the God my grandmothers, mother, pastor, Sunday school teachers, and preachers talked about, and the God I sang about—yet He was a familiar stranger to me.

There are people you generally know based on first impressions, casual, encounters, and what you learn about them from others. There are also those you come to trust— some based on their reputation and others because you know them well and have spent time with them, and so you understand their character and nature. I recognized God here and there throughout my life through many encounters and occasions. Sometimes I didn't even know it was Him. He revealed himself to us as Jehovah Jireh, our provider. At times He made a way for us through people we didn't expect it from. It may not have been the meal of portion of choice, or the provision of choice but it was something. My understanding was unfruitful because the key to a relationship with God is based on revelation and not by explanation.

I grew up in Boulevard Houses in East NY (ENY), Brooklyn. Each weekend we'd pack our bags and travel to Grandma Mae's house in order to spend quality time with the family, and to conveniently get to church for rehearsals, meetings, and other services. We had the best of both worlds with our family and friends in ENY and on Madison Street in Bushwick. Rugged Cross Baptist Church was where my family became pillars in ministry in their youth, and they still serve faithfully today. Over the years we grew in numbers rapidly. Rev. Moten really loved the youth, which is why we had youth and young adults of all ages in attendance and active in ministry every week. It all started for me in the storefront church at 928 Dekalb Avenue in Bedford-Stuyvesant (Bed-stuy), Brooklyn, where The Desha Moten Ensemble Choir, under the direction of Prof. Sherman Roberts, was the place to be!

I began singing in the sunbeam choir. There was something special about anniversaries in April. With my pink half-robe and burgundy skirt, soft big and frizzy naturally curly hair (wouldn't hold a good press), I'd sing and sit through a celebration like no other. Anyone who knows about choir anniversaries with no air conditioning, in a crowded church with standing room only, knows it can result in sweat and the greater possibility you will not look the same as when you went in.

Excitement filled the air as our home choirs prepared their best selections. Every visiting choir would pack the upstairs and downstairs with standing room only in order to experience this electric service! Can you hear the music? Can you feel the Spirit moving? Highlights of the anniversary were marching in to the hottest new gospel song of the season: brand new robes, the best lead singers, and the grand march. Oh my! The preparation alone would make you tired, however, the joy in the end was always so rewarding. Prof. Sherman L. Roberts Sr. was a teenager when he started playing the piano/organ. God truly anointed and appointed him as he developed the skills of his gifts to groom us, even in his youth. He taught us the discipline of ministry, singing, musicianship, giving God your best, and accountability. I believe he was an example that God can and will use a yielded vessel no matter how old they are.

Look at David and Jeremiah! I realized the gifts on my life while serving in ministry, leading numerous powerful songs where the presence of God would come in, yet I had the toughest time embracing it because of "the blues." Singing came naturally—a gift without formal training. We'd open our mouths like larks singing sweet melodies, most times without practice. I didn't appreciate my sound as a first soprano singing effortlessly. God's grace and mercy kept me! During times when I didn't understand why I resented the expensive price connected to my call and purpose—and as a creative person without proper outlets—running seemed like the answer. I figured God made a mistake choosing me as I didn't feel adequate enough. Stinking thinking will make you believe a lie before accepting the truth. I wasn't a mistake, my gift was special, and God wanted to use it for His glory and my good.

Church is the foundation upon which my life was built; my roots are rich and run deep. On Monday nights we'd have Bible study. We opened up by reciting the books of the Bible and foundational scriptures for Christian living. Wednesday nights was our regular prayer meeting which included devotional songs, scripture reading, and testimony time; it was an opportunity to share and acknowledge what God had done. Prayers rendered for specific situations encouraged many people. There were songs like, "Real, Real, Jesus is Real to Me," "I Get Joy When I Think About What He's Done For Me," hymns, and spiritual songs igniting power as we'd draw strength from one another. Even today, when I sing songs of praise to God, I'm empowered as I am reminded of my roots, where I come from, and who I am . . . and I will not be moved. I can't imagine what life would be like without my foundation in church. It saves my life!

Reflection

Did you grow up in church? If so, what was your experience like? If not, what was your foundation as a child? Are you a better person today as a result of your foundation?

Reflection Notes: _____

_____

_____

_____

_____

_____

_____

_____

_____

_____

_____

_____

_____

_____

_____

_____

Chapter 3

A Broken Road

Broken:
changing direction abruptly,
reduced fragments; torn,
not functioning properly; out of working order.

There's a saying, "If it ain't broke don't fix it." What happens when something is broken and in need of fixing but it takes more time, resources, and energy than expected? Denial of a things condition prevents an accurate assessment, while avoiding the problem creates more challenges, causing awkward moments to become the norm. Often, things break, and the level of damage determines the possibility for repair. Unfortunately, everything doesn't have the potential for repair. Thankfully, God is good at repairing and restoring! He's able to repair anyone and anything!

Masked issues left unchecked foster dysfunction. Hidden struggles cause the cycle called "suffering silently" to duplicate itself generationally. Not many are committed to the process of healthy change; some would rather settle comfortably, functioning within dysfunction and making inexcusable excuses for laziness, and perpetuating false humility in relationships. Culturally, we learn what we're free to talk about in public. Have you heard the saying, "What happens in my house, stays in my house" or "What happens in Vegas stays in Vegas"? This implies a secret code for anyone privy to activities considered risky, unethical, or immoral, one that remains only between the parties involved. Any form of abuse—especially in families—is taboo to discuss publicly. Defense mechanisms kicked in as a way to protect me from possible fake friendships, added hurt, and people conveniently using me. Sometimes when you're gifted, people are attracted to what you can do, and they disregard who you are. Often, I availed myself to repeat offenders while writing it off, when all the while it chipped away at me internally. How then could this brokenness be repaired when I was conditioned to receive whatever was given? Talk about unhealthy.

My parents were estranged off and on, and the view of a healthy marriage and relationship was not afforded me. I had no positive model by which to pattern my relationships in my home. While deep seeded roots of abandonment, rejection, insecurity, and needing to be accepted became a part of my foundation, anger unfortunately began to manifest in different ways. Both mom and dad were raised like me; they knew about God, could tell you about Him, yet there was a disconnect, in terms of the practical application of knowledge through understanding. The disconnect created a hole that only God could fill. It is crucial to the peace of an individual or environment to operate in order. Order is necessary! We learn throughout various stages of life what things mean based on social order. If there's a state of emergency, the television and radio stations will give a warning, with specific information on what safety precautions we are to adhere to. Sometimes in life we don't recognize the dangers or emergencies until crisis comes.

Ignoring the warning signs heightens the crisis, increasing the possibility of permanent disabilities. Playing the blame game didn't help Adam in the garden and it impedes progress.

Ultimately, brokenness was introduced to my family, leaving us in a place of desolation, hardship, dysfunction, chaos, poverty, despair, and uncovering. I questioned our situation many times, wondering why we experienced such adversity. I mean, we were good people, we didn't bother anyone, and we were respectful, church-going folks. What did we do to deserve this? I'm sure there were many families dealing with deeper things. I've never received a valid explanation because both mom and dad have different stories about what happened. However, in time I understood that God, the church, and our biological and extended families, became our escape and refuge. They are an oasis, the refilling station, a quiet stream (as referred to in Psalm 23), and our place to run to in order to make it through the week. I've heard it said that if you know better you do better. I beg to differ. Everyone has a will and the power to choose, and every choice is rooted in character. Ignoring the problem, giving in to the emotions, and succumbing to pressure, only makes things more challenging. Hope deferred truly makes the heart sick! What was the hope, where did it lie?

In my case, the unresolved issues regarding my estranged family opened the door to many things as I tried to fill the void reserved for Christ. I started dating at fifteen years old. Really? What did I know about dating with no clear view of what it should look like or who I was? The displacement of order plants seeds of disorder. With each struggle, this dysfunctional foundation—with cracks built in—began to cave in. Because my dad was not around or accessible, my then boyfriend (now husband) asked my mom for permission to date me. Go figure! Our families grew up together, so I'm sure that played a part in her being okay with me dating him. Communication between my boyfriend and I was limited, although he would visit for hours. Our time together was filled with silence, a little hugging, some kissing, and non-verbal dialogue. I mean what was I supposed to say? He knew I liked him and he liked me.

We wanted to spend time together and didn't want to be apart, but I was deficient in communication skills.

Brokenness was conveyed without intention. How could I give something I was deficient in? Ignorance is not just a choice, it's also learned behavior. He grew up in a home where his mom talked to him about any and everything! It was natural for him to expect more openness between us, and thankfully he helped me. This breakdown bothered him so much that he asked his mom to talk to me. I tell you, she talked, and listened, and talked some more. I appreciated it then and I still do today. I was uncomfortable with really personal things but grateful for her heart, wisdom, and openness.

Premarital sex was an epidemic plaguing the youth in my generation. Teen pregnancy was a symptom of deeper issues. Promiscuity introduced itself through curiosity. Sexual abuse had brought core challenges so deep, that it demanded time, commitment, truth, and discipline to maintain my deliverance and freedom.

As a teen, I was molested by a family member, which created in me more brokenness, defense mechanisms, and unchecked behavior. Memories of that night are in the forefront of my mind, replaying in slow motion.

One weekend while at my aunt and uncles, and in a deep sleep, I was awakened to the touch of an intruders hand in my panties, touching my special place. The place reserved only for my husband is now being fondled by an unauthorized male. In order for him to get to where I was, he slithered in the dark from his room, past his parents room, and crawled behind me in a bed I was sharing with my cousin . . . and he touched me.

How awful to wake up to such an invasive violation! I screamed, cried, and he slithered back into his room in the darkness, and no one said a word. What kind of dysfunctional, twisted, mess was that? Who knows of abuse yet acts like it never happened? What kind of a message does this send to the victim and predator? It was like knowing people were there but knowing they were not there. I carried anger, hurt, and confusion inside, and unforgiveness for years. Secrets will send you to the grave early, torment you in your silent moments, rob you of your future, and pervert purity and innocence. They will keep you from protecting others and potentially make you physically, emotionally, and mentally sick. The truth is there are so many family secrets not dealt with for the sake of protecting victims or "moving forward." Some predators are now preachers with licenses to help people, even though they should be registered sex offenders and not permitted to be within two feet of a child. Is that grace or stupidity on behalf of those responsible for stewardship? I'll always be an advocate. In order to be free the root must be identified, pulled up, and discarded.

On Jan 30, 1990 my life changed even more drastically. My cousins and I were cutting school when suddenly the phone rang. Who answers the house phone with no caller ID during school hours at a cutting school party? Malissa Smiley (now Redmond)! This phone call was not like any other call. This call shifted our lives forever. It was a police officer asking if anyone knew my grandmother, Ms. Della Mae Joyner. I stated she was my grandmother, and the officer let me know she was rushed to the hospital, and someone should meet them on the corner of Madison and Bushwick Avenue, and they'd take me to her. It was the first time we cut school and didn't get into trouble.

After hanging up the phone I told everyone to call their parents. Then I headed out the door full speed to the corner. I sprinted down the block with an NYPD van in view. Everything happened in slow motion, and it seemed like I'd never get there. The police were waiting for me. I got into the van, and they handed me her shopping bag she dropped when she fell.

Grandma had a doctor visit that morning and was on her way back. She must've stopped at the store first before making her way home. As we drove to Woodhull Hospital, my mind raced, my heart palpitated, and my stomach churned at the thought of something being wrong with Grandma. I looked through the bag of groceries and there were things in there that I couldn't understand why she bought. Grandma Mae fussed a lot but she loved even harder.

I remembered back to when my parents had threatened to send me away because I was a truant, but Grandma sat me on the edge of her bed and talked to me, listening to my heart and giving me an opportunity to see things in a better light without frustration. Reflecting on our conversation, I never could have imagined what happened next. I got to the hospital, and they took me to a waiting area where two doctors in white coats came into the room saying, "I'm sorry, we did all we could do." I've seen this on TV, but I couldn't imagine this being real life. Broken is an understatement. At age sixteen, I had the responsibility of identifying my grandma's body. A day that started out with carefree fun was now filled with trauma and sadness. They took me in where she laid. Her tooth shifted and there was a little blood on her mouth from the fall. I've never cried like that in my life. Honestly, I still cry. We didn't have a home telephone so I had to call the Harrison's, our earthly angels, in order to get the message to my mom. All the while I was waiting for my family to come to the hospital. Everything after that day seemed like it didn't matter. My grandma was no longer here. The helplessness overwhelmed me because there was nothing I could do to change it. I remember a poem on her kitchen wall that read, "God grant me the serenity to accept the things I cannot change." In this situation, I knew. It's a blur but my heart still aches.

At age seventeen, I became pregnant with our first child. What did I know about raising a baby when I was a child myself? My son, Davon, became the push I needed to press through the fragmented life I knew. His birth gave me a sense of significance again. Our little guy weighed in at five pounds, two ounces, and stretched in at sixteen inches long, with skin bright as the sun, a peanut-shaped head, and a buzz cut. Giving birth naturally was incredible! I'm still in awe at the wonders of God and how he designed women to bring forth life. This process opened a whole new world to me, teaching me that my choices have consequences that affect not only me. I've learned that the answer to a problem is always a person. That someone will be a source and a resource to get you to where you need to be or to connect you through networking. Davon connected me to a love I never knew between parents and children. I became a mother but I realized I stopped being a daughter. While I was pregnant with Davey, I transitioned to a pregnant teen school to try and finish my high school education strong.

The guidance counselor was very supportive and helped me get back on track. I was lost and needed help finding my way. After having Davey, I went to Brooklyn Comprehensive Night High School in order to finish with a flex schedule. Mr. Azeez, my math teacher, saw something in me I didn't believe about myself. He said, "Malissa, go straight to college and don't wait; you can do it!" (spoken in my African voice). Many times the scales on your eyes will cloud your view and others will see the potential and power in you to soar. It's not about what others see or believe but what you believe and respond to. Thank God I graduated high school with my diploma and honors in mathematics. With determination, focus, and support, I did it! Procrastination is a thief! It robbed me blind and paralyzed me. There were indicators pointing me in the right direction,

21

but ignoring counsel kept me cycling poor outcomes. The church girl was having a baby, singing in the choir, struggling with self-esteem, experiencing brokenness in dating, confused about the hardships and secrets in the family of sexual abuse, angry, suicidal, blaming everyone for her condition, and she had no real peace. Who could I really turn to with no worries of judgment or of people spreading my business? Trust issues were an understatement! I couldn't even trust myself. I felt like God didn't love me anymore because I messed up. How wrong I was and I didn't know it. Nothing could be further from the truth, and no one or nothing can compare to the Father's love.

By age nineteen, I was having our second child, still singing in the choir, struggling at home, and instead of reaching for God, I ran as fast as I could, disconnecting my heart from every church experience. I was existing but not living, and on my way to my first apartment with no real life or relationship skills. Now I was broken and bitter with depression as an anchor, and a defense mechanism of walls keeping everyone out as I trapped myself in. How far could I really run? Psalm 139:7 states, "Where can I go from your Spirit? Where can I flee from your presence?" There was no excuse for not knowing God except refusing to choose him daily. Even today, my family is filled with ordained pastors, ministers, praise & worship leaders, musicians, and recording artists on both sides of the family. The matriarchs represented courage, strength, peace, struggle, fortitude, phenomenal cooking, togetherness, correction, women of God, and the list goes on. Even when the unthinkable manifested there was nothing like a good church to attend, prayer, and a good old family meeting to get things back in order. It was our way of dealing with things and by the grace of God we made it through! Shotgun weddings were performed. Some of the marriages are nonexistent today or on the verge of ending. Conforming to a culture that manipulated scripture to justify inconsistencies, became the standard.

On May 21, 1994, I was married to my husband Derrick. At twenty years old I was married, with two beautiful children (the best of both worlds: a boy and a girl), and our own place. God blessed the broken road we were on and is still blessing us now. Marriage is more than preparing for a glorious day with beautiful moments, expensive memories, and a large crowd witnessing the covenant between two people and God. God ordained marriage with the intention of it lasting until death. Nowadays, couples in preparation for marriage have premarital classes. We were not afforded that opportunity, and we realize the importance of counsel before making such a serious commitment. Not long after we were married, Rev. Moten, our spiritual father, went home to be with the Lord. It was the absolute worst time for our church! Division, confusion, backbiting, and anything you can think of was taking place. It seemed like the biggest break up in a family. People began to leave the church. The leadership shifted and unfortunately we went through a dry wilderness.

The church is the body of believers and is not limited to the building we fellowship in. Being a part of the church is who we are identified with in our lifestyle, because of a relationship with God through the Lordship of Christ Jesus. As believers we are responsible for growing in grace. Grace is unmerited favor.

God knew I needed to be planted in Rugged Cross! The fundamentals I learned help me today to stay grounded; I thank God for my upbringing in the Baptist church. My oldest sister attended a church called CLC (Christian Life Centre) with the blessing of pastor Moten before he expired. Although she often invited me, I would only attend on Tuesday nights because of my responsibilities to serve on Sundays at RCBC as a choir director, lead soloist, Sunbeam Choir Supervisor, and a full fledge member. Visiting made me realize that I needed so much more! Of course my roots were deep in the Baptist church, but my decision to seek for more attracted me to the depth in teaching. I figured no one knew me, and I could start fresh and exist in the crowd, with no responsibilities except worshipping God, getting the much needed word, and avoiding the possibilities of drama through service to and with "church people." After all, I didn't have to participate in any group to serve God. Church hurt is a different type of hurt, and I'd had my share, got the t-shirt, and gave it back! Every Tuesday became a greater drawing for me as I listened with intensity to every word spoken, prayers prayed, or songs sung. In a room full of people, it seemed like God was speaking directly to me. Have you ever experienced that? I felt good inside. I felt like I was naked, as if everyone knew God was telling my business through this man I'd never seen before. Character development is important! Dealing with real issues is urgent! The church is a hospital for the sick, so we must manage our expectations and maintain a healthy perspective in order to live a balanced life. I believe God needed me in RCBC, and sent me to sit in CLC under the leadership of Dr AR Bernard and Pastor Karen to save my life and help me develop in character, not just in my gifting: practical teaching for everyday living.

What an incredible mandate! Who would think that God would choose to use someone like me? Can anything good come from ENY, Brooklyn? I wondered what would become of the fragments of my life.

Thankfully, I embraced my assignment knowing I am a woman with a relevant word articulating it with grace, accuracy, power, and authority through song and teaching! Ultimately, God uses everything to work for my good (Romans 8:28-29)! Although the truth hurts, it's liberating! Don't despise small beginnings even though you don't understand them. There's a song I like to listen to by a group called Rascal Flatts, called, "Bless the Broken Road." It tells the story of someone on a journey finding love by way of a broken road. Sometimes you can find what you need while traveling through uncomfortable situations.

After all, it was in my broken place I found my husband. It was also there that I found my voice and purpose again. Most importantly, I found out that God loves me, will never leave me, and is committed to my process, so it's okay to be committed too.

Reflection

Here is a poem I wrote to help me in the uprooting process:

Advocate

I wish I could forget what I've been through.

However, the scars constantly remind me of the bars that confined me.

My heart glum, feeling numb, needing an escape.

There's nowhere to run!

The self inflicted psychological wounds rehearsed in unending scenes of events are more vivid with each play.

Frame by frame the replays are more real and horrific!
In slow motion . . . molestation, rape, or any type of abuse can be an absolute nightmare!

How could someone do this? How can someone know of the infractions against you and not help?

Why would anyone ignore the cry of one in need of desperate rescue?

I recall it like it was yesterday.

All of a sudden the snake slithering on the ground crawls in the bed I'm in and imposes himself on me.

Awakened by the violation I scream, hit, cry, nothing moves . . . I'm not alone so I'm confused at the fact that no one helps.

The silence is so loud while I'm ignored and needing someone, anyone to take action or say STOP! I mean really, are you gonna be that one who has eyes to see but doesn't see? Hear something but turn a deaf ear to it? Perpetuate cycles you were exposed to and subject me to it?

This arrogant demon crawls out of the bed and onto the floor to go back to the hell he came from.

I'm in disbelief with tears streaming down my face. I ponder the idea that maybe I was responsible for this disruption of peace.

Somehow I get through the night. Morning comes and no one bothers to ask if I'm ok. It seemed like the norm. I wonder who else shares my new experience as well.

Anger is now the foundation by which I deal with the things dealt to me. The defenses are up!

Years later I'm confronted with this same demon all grown up who asks me, "Why did you say anything?" Then he proceeds to threaten me with more perversion.

What the hell? Yes, hell!

The uncanny audacity of a predator is disgusting! Subtlety is a joke, talk about blatant flagrant fouls.

Without hesitation I respond saying, "I was supposed to say something, and no you won't!"

Hmmm, once a victim, now forever an advocate!

Tell if someone's hurt you, touched you inappropriately, is harassing you, or makes you feel uncomfortable. An injustice to one is an injustice to everyone.

Don't suffer silently, downloading viruses, causing your memory to be damaged beyond repair.

Reflection Notes: _____

Chapter 4

Double Entendre

Double Entendre:
a phrase, saying, or sentence that can be interpreted in two different ways.

The church can be a place of refreshing or it can be a place of refining.

Self-sufficiency and independence are two of the most common factors driving our nation. Folks strive to get their piece of the pie. Sadly, people are hurting while in pursuit of their happiness, or pseudo-happiness. Corporate America is known for their crab mentality. Many successful people have worked diligently climbing the ladder at the expense of others, not caring about those who get in their way. I mean as long as they get results it doesn't matter how they're getting the job done. Sadly enough, this mentality has filtered its way into the church. Yes, the church has become a breeding ground for the dog-eat-dog world. Clergy, musicians, and layman alike are sometimes guilty of fostering and cosigning the sowing of discord among the brethren, beautifying it with flattering words and filthy hearts. Proverbs 14:12 (*NLT*) states, "There is a path before each person that seems right, but it ends in death." This text is not limited to physical death but also includes death in relationships, communication, and freedom.

There are controversies all over the world. We observe them in entertainment, education, government, and communities. Each is affected differently. Unfortunately, they also happen in the world we know as church. Yes, church! I said it! Who could imagine that the house of worship, place of refuge, and haven for the hurting could very well be a lion's den (the habitation of wild animals). Although there are few open discussions about these challenges and books on the subject, there's also denial of its existence and turning a blind eye, but that does not mean it doesn't coexist within the building of the kingdom. The wheat and the tear grow together. If there were books, workshops, or tutorials called, *Church for Dummies, Discernment for Prey, Balance for the Super Spiritual*, or *Politics in Church*, it would be easier to navigate within the system victoriously, and truly see growing, healthy relationships with peers and especially with God. Hosea 4:6 (*NKJV*) states, "My people are destroyed for lack of knowledge." Wake up! Watch as well as pray!

In efforts to educate anyone interested in learning about anything, there are books available to take you through fundamentals on various subjects such as: *Accounting for Dummies, Computer for Dummies, Piano for Dummies*, etc. Of course, they're not implying that those in need of the information are dummies. They are practical guides and anyone can learn "how to" do a particular thing. This chapter is a snippet of what I'd call *Church for Dummies*.

Church for Dummies is a brief guide to inform people about what to expect from the church and church goers, how to address situations, and healthy tips. This will help you manage expectations, equipping you to overcome obstacles both expected and unexpected. Also, this tool is designed to empower a balanced walk with God and humanity. God created man to worship Him! Do you agree? A heart filled with gratitude responds in adoration to a loving God. Worship is a feeling of profound love and admiration. It is also a way to show devotion. The church—also known as the house of worship—is the place where people of various cultures, ages, and walks of life fellowship with God and one another. Common practices are prayer, praise, worship, and teachings about God and His unfailing, unconditional love for human kind. Jesus taught about true worship to a woman interested in the physical place where her ancestors worshipped (John 4:24). Though she was privately exposed about her lifestyle, she certainly was moved by Jesus' authenticity and gentleness, and by the power in his words. Therefore, she shared her experience with others. There are different facets of worship and each culture influences the interpretation thereof. Worship is not a slow song during service that makes people cry. Music is a tool used in worship; however, it's a matter of the heart. If there is no music, worship can still happen.

The members of the body of Christ have been called to be living examples of Christ-likeness. Sharing the message of love and hope with everyone you come in contact with is fundamental. The power in your witness is manifested through walking in agreement with the infallible word of God. The value of our witness is determined by integrity, obedience, consistency, and submission both in private and in public. Jesus purchased the salvation for "whosoever," through his blood on the cross, which means believers/Christians are not their own. Through the divine plan of God, access is granted, freedom is provided, and the abundant life is made available here and now. The order of services varies in denominations, based on their interpretation of faith. Denominations include but are not limited to Anglican, Baptist, Pentecostal, Presbyterian, Episcopalian, Seventh Day Adventist, and the list goes on. The word of God is a guide that can help us to design church services, function as individual believers, and work together as a corporate body. Prayer, praise, worship, teaching, preaching, Holy Communion, baby dedications, home-going services, water baptisms, and weddings are all integral parts of the experience that one may observe and or participate in, within a house of worship service.

We, like Christ, are not of this world, yet the world's culture can be found in some churches all over the world. There's a fine line between being relevant to those we're trying to reach and conforming to the world. It takes discernment, a righteous indignation, and wisdom to respond in a Christ like mature manner to maintain order and respect in the house of worship. Jesus checked improper behavior in the temple. He wasn't super spiritual and He did not diminish the power or validity of His ministry to the people by His demonstration. His love and reverence for the Father superseded the opinions of man. There was no room to tolerate inappropriate exchanges in the place of worship.

Jesus entered the temple area and drove out all who were buying and selling there. He overturned the tables of the money changers and the benches of those selling doves. He said, "It is written, 'My house will be called a house of prayer,' but you have made it a 'den of thieves'" (Matthew 21:12-13 *NKJV*). It takes courage, tenacity, and wisdom to speak up, speak out, and stand up for anything.

Familiarity opened the door to one thing I faced that almost caused me to walk away from the very thing I was born to do. With good intentions and the right heart, your good can be evil spoken of by deceptive people who present themselves as friends. Wolves come in sheep's clothing. My love for music and ministry developed throughout my life. The gifts I've been blessed with opened many doors but none compared to the assignment of a praise and worship leader. It was there that I found joy in the midst of the challenges at home or even at church, while encouraging and empowering the people to engage the heart of God through unrestrained praise and authentic worship. I've been blessed to co-labor with some of the most incredible singers and musicians, some of whom I still call friends. As a writer, it's great when you can synergize musically, creating music and a sound that embodies the beautiful love of God.

One day while in preparation for Tuesday night service, I received a call from the keyboard player asking to speak to me in his office. I gathered my things and made my way downstairs from my office to his. My mind was focused on the assignment at hand, but what happened next shook me to the core. His greeting was familiar but then he began to share that he was developing "romantic feelings" for me. My heart sank. I was off the market . . . married with children, he was as well; yet something strange took place in his mind and heart that I was oblivious to. He'd never made me feel uncomfortable in any way, so this truly came out of left field. As friends, we would get a bite to eat, and as musicians we spent many hours arranging, recording, and creating, but here we are getting ready for service and sadly the relationship is forever changed. His secret is out and I can't ignore it or leave it unaddressed. I communicate my apologies for his feelings, clearly defining the boundaries, and left the office. I called one of my friends, who happened to share that this same person was a bit too familiar with her. I didn't judge him based on what she said, but I felt horrible and I didn't do anything wrong. I called my husband, and told him what happened. He said, "Did he touch you? If not, it's ok and we'll talk about it when you get home." I still had the task of preparing for service. While ironing my skirt, I burned it being nervous from what I just experienced, and I felt like leaving and never coming back. Somehow I made it though the service, standing in one place. Anyone who knows me knows that I like to walk while ministering. That night my feet were cemented to the floor, my mind raced, and I was crying out to God within myself.

33

The next day was an early day. We prepared for chapel with the staff. Here I am again leading and the same keyboard player is playing. With that stupid grin on his face, he was relieved and I felt so violated. After chapel, I asked to speak with him to confirm his message from the day before, redefine the relationship, and move forward knowing that we can no longer be friends or greet each other with any physical contact. Why me? What in the world is this? Who would've thought I'd be faced with this at church? This may be the norm for some but he found out that I wasn't the one. This familiarity between him and the other young lady ended when she left on December 31st. I jokingly said to her, "You know that spirit will need someone to attach to and it won't be me!" On January 2nd of that New Year, lo and behold . . . it tried but didn't succeed. On top of that we had to have a tribunal. I had never felt more humiliated than to be in a meeting where lies are told and exposed. My reputation and name were in question because of a selfish, perverted, lying, unfaithful, and deceiving man hiding behind his gifts but with no character. Even until this day, some people believed his lies; they blame me for him no longer working at his job, and they don't speak to me. God knows the truth and I'm grateful the accusations fell to the ground, because truth vindicated me.

Unfortunately, dealing with sexual harassment in the workplace is more common than not. This is church! My trust went out the door and I've never been the same relationally.

Through our words we worship, praise, pray, affirm, edify, build up, create, and tear down. Words are so powerful! Death and life is in your mouth. The enemy is silencing those who need to speak up—who are suffering through their silence, battling depression, and tormented daily. Secrets, lies, taboos, fears, insecurities, uncertainties, and not wanting to deal with repercussions will keep the silence going. Silence is golden when necessary. Ecclesiastes 3 (NIV) states it best, "There's a time for everything"! Knowing the seasons and the times is crucial for growth and for precision in being prudent. It's time to be bold and speak up! Stand up for righteousness! I can only imagine what went through Jesus' mind when he came into the temple and saw what was taking place. It was the spirit and motivation behind the acts that raised the holy indignation. Such arrogance and pride; monopolizing opportunities in the house of God. The house of worship was disrespected and Jesus expressed His disapproval. We too should have the same outlook, no longer tolerating the intolerable. It's like someone coming into your home and setting up their own agendas, disregarding you as if they have the right and you can just flow with it. By no means will you tolerate such nonsense in your home, so it is necessary for accountability to such foolishness in our churches. Double standards have no place in the church; even God is no respecter of persons. Though there is indeed transformation taking place, souls being saved, and lives are changing, simultaneously many hearts are conflicted because of some representations of Christ.

Jesus performed many miracles. One miracle he's still performing is healing the dumb so that they may speak. Your words have creative power, bringing into existence exactly what you say. God created through releasing words with power. After He created He reflected, declaring it was good.

How many of you can say that you watch carefully what you say, speaking with intention for positive results? If you had the chance to take back something you've said, would you? If so, what would it be? If you had the chance to say things you should have said but didn't at the time, what would it be and why?

If you see something, say something! Say something to the right people! Who are the right people? I'm glad you asked . . .

First, pray, asking for guidance regarding what to do and whom you should share it with. Second, make sure you have solid information and not just speculation or strong emotions. Third, find someone who is mature and trustworthy. Let your words—filled with power—release the positive in place of the negative. Be a conduit of influence that glorifies God in all that you do and say.

To the ones challenged with issues, weaknesses, insecurities, fear, and lack of confidence . . . be encouraged. The devil tries to create distractions, diverting attention from God, directing focus to the possible challenges or actual issues within any house of worship. He also uses people! It's always a fight for territory! Having peace does not mean you can avoid uncomfortable situations; however, you're blessed with the advantage of knowing God sees, knows, cares, and will never leave you to yourself. The Holy Spirit is the best teacher! He will certainly bring truth, and truth will open the doors to freedom, even if it hurts. Some experiences in church with church people can cloud your view of God. There's no perfect individual, family, corporation, community, or church. It takes maturity and work to maintain a healthy perspective. The church God knows is a refreshing rain, a lifeline, the place where He dwells, meeting people at their point of need, and escorting them higher.

Mismanaged expectations of the church and representatives can deter you from committing to public service in church. Unresolved issues within the church are poisonous roots and it is our responsibility to communicate the truth in love, administering the love of Christ. With freedom comes responsibility. It is not the will of God for anyone to be depressed, abused, or diminished in intrinsic worth. We have a duty to protect and serve one another, building each other, and expanding the ministry through our specific gifts.

Who is taking responsibility for their freedom? John 8:32 (*NIV*) states, "Then you will know the truth, and the truth will set you free." Truth can be painful but definitely liberating. Through personal development, ownership, and commitment, the church can truly reflect light and love.

Because the battlefield is in the mind, we often focus on the enemy outside instead of the enemy within, and more of our victories are experienced alone.

There's not enough room in the heart for love and hate. There's not enough space in the mind for confusion and peace. There's not enough time to waste on unfruitful opportunities.

Discernment will save you from investing yourself in substitutes of the promises, due to impatience, ignorance, and disobedience.

Don't let people label you because they don't care enough to love you through your process or they don't know what they're talking about! Grief is not only experienced when losing a loved one. Many people are grieving and don't know it or acknowledge it. You can be healed, comforted, strengthened, and free from the pain of grief . . . God is able!

When I went through my time of grieving, these words came to mind, and I considered them in my heart:

"Lay me at the throne, leave me there alone" (from the song, "Take Me to the King").

I'm not moody or a diva . . . I'm grieving (so please don't judge me or think you know all that is going on with me).

Wait on The Lord and be of good courage! Choose life!

Reflection

Have you overcome a difficult situation only to find out that the process was necessary although it was painful? If so, what was the situation and how did you overcome it?

Reflection Notes: _____

_____

_____

_____

_____

_____

_____

_____

_____

_____

_____

_____

_____

_____

_____

_____

Chapter 5

Discernment

Discernment:
acuteness of judgment and understanding.

An example of a child's curiosity is when they touch a stove; at first it seems to the child to be an amazing time of discovery— only until they find out that it gets *hot*! Children have no awareness of hidden danger and can be fearless. Their trust is in those who care for them; adults are responsible for teaching what is safe and unsafe. This teaching includes but is not limited to places, things, family, friends of the family, and so on. Some people can detect trouble before it comes; they may even become frustrated when they don't have proof of what they are sensing. Not enough people make such determinations quickly and adjust accordingly. Like a lioness on the prowl, so are individuals driven by greed, power, and lust, preying on the naïve who have no clue about the possibilities of danger. Like the antelope enjoying the day are those who go through life singing "Hakuna Matata," from *The Lion King*, not knowing they're being set up for destruction. Most of the time, it is at the hands of the ones they know, trust, or even love.

I've often wondered why family secrets are passed on from generation to generation, without allowing a severing of the cycle by exposing the spirit and the dysfunction of these secrets. Proverbs 4:7 says to get wisdom, but in all of your getting, get understanding. Life and relationships should be taken seriously, and with balance. Often, the exposure we have experienced and grown accustomed to shapes our view of the world, ourselves, and God. With the desire of my elders to protect the younger ones from what was considered grown-up information, a gap was created in communication. Vital dialog and actions could have stopped molestation, physical abuse, mental abuse, and social isolation. As I reflect, if I had the opportunity to interview my biological and extended family about their experiences growing up, I imagine they would share a few secrets. Some of their experiences were likely due to poor judgment, low self esteem, and past abuses—including both mental and sexual abuse. But God and his grace kept us even when we didn't discern the environment, people, or situations.

Discernment is key in balancing healthy spaces in relationships. Qualifying healthy space takes maturity, integrity, good character, and consistency. You can't fake fruit! Here's a word to the wise: you can only pretend for so long because the real you will come out, slowly but surely! Maya Angelou said, "When people show you who they are, believe them!" Make the adjustment and keep moving forward.

Once I began the healing process of being delivered from the opinions of others, settling issues of abandonment, and being accepted, my days didn't seem as long. Remembering went from a full blown movie to sneak previews and clips. I often expended great energy trying to convince myself of a false reality, and I therefore provided a disservice to God, myself, and others.

I've learned that the healing process hurts more than the initial infliction of a wound, but with God's help, positive support, and determination, you can really live the life of an overcomer.

As an advocate who educates others on abuse while empowering victims young and mature in age, I experience such joy knowing that cycles are being broken. Exposing these negative behaviors provides opportunities to head off both potential abuse and abusers. If you have the opportunity to warn someone of danger, take responsibility and do so! You can save a life from ruin. The predator, motivated by lust and many other creepy things, is constantly discerning opportunities to manipulate situations. Lust is a powerful motivator to the predators. Trust with a potential victim can be built with false smiles, illegitimate experiences, insincere conversation, and flattery of the tongue.

Abuse is not limited to any form of sex! Abuse is the abnormal use of anything, thereby bringing harm to the victim. Wake up! Pay attention! Read between the lines! Check the fine print! Don't drink the Kool-aid! The unspoken things are telling you something! "Watch and pray so that you will not fall into temptation. The spirit is willing, but the flesh is weak" (Matthew 26:41 *NIV*).

When Jesus was preparing for His death, He went to the Garden of Gethsemane. Peter, James, and John accompanied Him while He prayed. He gave them instructions to keep watch with Him, meaning for them to pay attention (also to pray) while He went and prayed. They fell asleep while on post and Jesus woke them two times. When He finished praying the last time, He told them to keep sleeping because His betrayer, Judas, had come. I can't imagine the fatigue the disciples experienced. However, out of all the disciples called to follow Jesus, He took only the three of them into the intimate place with Him. What an honor to be on post while the Messiah travailed in prayer, alone with the Father. The position of watching and praying has not changed. As a matter of fact, it's imperative now more than ever! Some have gotten off their posts with no relief. Where are the watchmen, the intercessors, the discerners, and the prudent? Right now, Jesus is in heaven making intercession for us. What are we doing? Are we sleeping on post?

Listen up! The time is now to disarm and dismantle some ideas and perceptions regarding the church, churchgoers, leaders, musicians, singers, staff (servers), Christians, and the like. Unregistered offenders are dangerously on the prowl and some are hidden in churches. Ignorance has plagued so many because there's a great need to believe that there is a place of refreshing with no flaws or challenges . . . a place to make exchanges in the presence of God through attending services and receiving counsel, assistance, restoration and renewal. Assumptions can sometimes be wrong, such as, people who attend church are Christ-like, led by the Holy Spirit, have an endearing relationship with God, pray, love all people, and are kind hearted and patient.

That's not based on truth but on a false sense of reality. I've heard about and met a few who call themselves "Christians/believers," but they're the meanest, most arrogant, indignant, rude, impatient, will-cuss-you-out-and-pray-later humans one could come across. Can we be honest? These folks give Christ—not Christians—a bad rap because of lack of discipline, insubordination, and selfishness, frustrating the grace extended to them in order to satisfy the flesh. Stereotypes in all forms offer only extremes, yet due to the first impression from poor representations (whether a company, corporation, organization, business, class, ethnic group, or gender) stereotypic classifications are the standard.

Allow the truth to set you free! What is the truth? The truth is, people are people no matter the title, call, assignment, gift, or place. Some people are gifted to do great works. Just because someone has a position of power and authority does not mean they are competent or integral.

Take a look at every sphere of influence. Many things have come to the light, having been viewed with a microscope to delve into the crevices; some things bring resolution and others

42

only a glimpse in that direction, unveiling just enough to stimulate thought and conversation. The media and magazines have the job of dictating what we buy, wear, and eat. In the process, they impose these ideas from folks who may have a dimmed world view, who have self-esteem issues just like everyone who is influenced by them; but the consumer doesn't know that. Understanding the need for healthy and balanced relationships, good communication, and managing your personal and professional life is crucial whether you're a person of faith or not. Deep-seated issues can go down even deeper if not addressed, invoking selfish desires, thoughtlessness, reckless behavior, and desensitizing us. Dislocation, denial, deceit, and betrayal become character traits that replace loyalty, trust, and true love when unfiltered negativity is granted permission to not just pass through the mind, but take a "rent free" space in your mind and heart. It's good to know others; however, knowing yourself is the greater of the two. Make sure you're incubating the right things; filter them through the Holy Spirit, and don't let anything paralyze you with fear, excuses, pity, regret, hurt, or rejection.

There were days when I'd look in the mirror and all I could see was pain, hurt, rejection, and the cares of life. My heart condition was frail, irregular, and weak due to hope deferred. All it took to be on a better path was a lot of love, consistent reminders through the Word of God, and the willingness to be healed. The healing process reminds you of the wounds. For me, it was harder to remember what the truth was than it was to forget the lies. Now, I look in the mirror through a balanced filter.

The things I can change, I work on. The things I can't change, I pray about. I am moving forward. My best days are here!

Helpful Tips

- The spirit of manipulation, control, and Jacob seek opportunities to advance at the expense of the weak, innocent, needy, insecure, lazy, procrastinating, and fearful. They classify the opportunity as "looking out for their best interests" while really being motivated by ego, the need to be in control, and having the upper hand.

- There's nothing wrong with being skillful at what you do; however, it should not be at the cost of the weak. Some say it's survival of the fittest; only the strong survive, and in the world, it's expected and accepted.

- Pay close attention to those closest to you—those who have access to you both directly and indirectly. Anyone could have an agenda.

- Don't ignore or disregard the gut feeling because of a lack of understanding. Pray, and ask for discernment and wisdom to respond if and when necessary.

- Sticking together does not mean condoning or supporting negative behavior.

- Pretending things don't exist does not make them go away.

- Enablers tend to pacify situations that are in great need of correction because of double standards and/or fear.

- The individual and/or the situation will have an effect on the outcome.

- Offenders don't deserve the same space and value they had in your life before, unless through time they demonstrate growth and remorse, and they are not perpetual violators.

- Standing for truth and righteousness doesn't mean you'll have support. As a matter of fact, it can be very lonely.

- When discernment is in operation wisdom is there.

- The greatest help you can sometimes be to others is to give them totally to God!

- Find the healthy balance where truth is expressed, forgiveness is evident, and the process of reconciliation is in operation.

Reflection

God is the common thread in my life. Despite all of the challenges, I decided to commit to the process of growth and maturation. His presence is evident throughout the journey and His promise to never leave nor forsake me is what I continue to stand on.

Take a look at your life and reflect. Write down your thoughts.

Reflection Notes: _____

_____

_____

_____

_____

_____

_____

_____

_____

_____

_____

_____

Chapter 6

Assess Yourself

Assess:

to estimate officially the value of.

to fix.

to estimate or judge the value; character evaluation.

Assessments are essential in experiencing true growth. Whether in a marriage, business, family, or organization, within each season it's important to pay attention. Often, we invest more of ourselves in others, things, work, and the like, keeping busy while losing pieces of ourselves through poor management. Without truthful self evaluations, you can't determine the current condition or make necessary changes for the greater good. These evaluations are administered by employers quarterly or annually, to review employees and their job performance, and to gain statistics. This process is in place to ensure quality control, customer care, productivity, management, and maintaining growth.

The gift is connected to the giver as character is connected to the individual. It's often evident that character development in some people is not as important to them as how they look outwardly—in the eyes of others. Throughout the stages and levels of life, you will find that avoiding the tough decisions are more common than not. The energy and work needed for balanced development doesn't go over well with impatient, controlling, lazy, overachievers. There is a great need for commitment to the process and not just glorying in the grand finale. There are those who—for many reasons—live with beams in their own eyes while feeling more responsible for the specks in the eyes of others. No matter how long it takes to reach a goal, you cannot skip steps expecting the end result to yield fruit that remains.

Depression is a thief! It robs you of time, energy, opportunities, relationships, and dreams. Years ago I wrote a song entitled, "Don't Let the Vision Die." This song was birthed at a time when my rose colored glasses clouded my view of seeing things as they really were. My opportunities to use stumbling blocks as stepping stones were dimmed, due to hope deferred, especially since I saw hurt, pain, rejection, and injustice. My mind was swallowed up with negative thoughts; I expected bad things to happen, because they often did!

As a dreamer, reading Habakkuk 2:2-3 put a lot of things into perspective for me. I wrote my first song when I was twelve years old. Writing was one of the creative outlets that allowed me a way of expressing that I couldn't communicate otherwise. When it comes to birthing a vision or a dream, there are fundamental stages you must grow through. By being clear in my vision, I eliminated the possibilities of being distracted by counterfeits. Pressing forward wasn't as painful. I realized it took planning, preparation, courage, discipline, focus, people, and faith to bring dreams and vision into fruition. Sharing dreams with just anyone can cause you to miscarry, abort, or give birth prematurely.

As a mother of four beautiful children with my husband of twenty-two years, I've learned that each child has different needs, and each pregnancy has its own story. I was high risk with all of my children, and high risk pregnancies are no joke! Pre-term labor reoccurred in every pregnancy. I carried the first three for eight months and the last one made it to the first week of the ninth month. My mom and I had this in common: we both have four children, one boy and three girls; our sons were first; and we carried the first three children eight months and the last child nine months. Premature babies come with unexpected risks. My oldest and knee baby were hospitalized after birth, but thank God they're doing well today.

While writing this book—a three year process—I often wondered what the end would be; could I really do it and would it benefit others? Assessing myself is the greatest decision I've made toward building healthier relationships, healthy expectations, owning my truth, and changing outcomes. Every opportunity that is presented is not from God! Motives are important! Unfortunately, I was deceived a few times, and I gave grace to some who needed a judgment, and in so doing I accepted the counterfeit (an "opportunity" dressed in sheep's clothing, which only delayed the process). Please don't get me wrong . . . some things spoken by God through people require testing. This book has certainly been tried, as have my music and ministry! I'm determined to commit to the process and not just to the end thereof. Although the journey is filled with challenges, unexpected turns, losses, and risks, I believe that when God says "Go, I got this and you," I go!

Gifts create room where there is no door. I recall working at a school in Bushwick, Brooklyn, where my children attended since ages two and a half. This school was a pillar in the community for numerous years, building strong foundations for children and their families through child care. The programs offered were solid, with staff members who were like family. The school director created a position for me as an Arts Consultant, which entailed teaching music, drama, and dance, pioneering the program and designing lesson plans to complement the overall department. She saw something in me that I knew I had, and it opened a door that blessed the community as well as me and my family. Yes! What was offered to me was something that was never done before. *RoundTable*

Child Care Center, which is now just a memory due to politics and its closing in 2012, afforded me the opportunity to share my gifts, inspire children, and become a part of history in the community.

Singing, dancing, and acting are my natural gifts. My mother prayed that God would send someone into our lives to teach us musically, and He answered her prayer through Professor Sherman Roberts. It is through the singing gift that I discovered my assignments in life, and although many times I didn't want to use it, I realized that it was the doorway to many other assignments. Today, it is my singing gift that is used most in reaching the masses, encouraging folks. I've traveled the world singing the gospel of Jesus Christ. To name a few, I've been to Italy, Australia, Austria, England, the Bahamas, Aruba, and to many places throughout the United States. I sang on many stages, acted in off-Broadway plays, and met many wonderful people along the way. The most rewarding moments are when I remember that everything that happened or happens in my life is being used for my good, even when it doesn't look like it. God chose me to do what I do! That is the greatest, most liberating blessing! Using my God-given abilities is what qualifies me as an overcomer. Impatience while waiting for the manifestation of a dream is dangerous. It is through doing what I've been called, anointed, and appointed to do consistently that enables my assessments of the bigger picture—and the details—to be balanced.

"Balance is emotional and mental steadiness."
-Bishop T.D. Jakes.

Choosing to be a better you is up to you!
The awesome thing is, you can't do it all alone, and help is within your reach if it's needed. Pride may keep you from

asking, and fear may paralyze you from reaching out, but God will never give you an assignment that's impossible to complete. Courage is necessary, discipline is key, consistency is powerful, and determination is empowering. Isolation from things and people as a defense mechanism will enable you. Isolating problems while developing and protecting the good is integral in achieving goals.

According to the scripture, when sin entered through Adam in the garden, God asked "Where are you?" I believe this was the first evaluation/assessment with mankind in order to get things back on track. It wasn't a literal question; it was more a question pertaining to the fallen condition of man. Elohim never intended for man to experience ruin through sin. As a matter of fact, his foreknowledge and love for humanity demanded a response through Jesus Christ's offering.

Anytime you choose anything that takes you away from your original purpose, it's a serious situation and a fallen condition, which requires an assessment by you or possibly by others in order to get back on track.

The healing process hurts more than the infliction of a wound. So grow while going through it.

Reflection

Writing is therapeutic!
Praying is therapeutic!
Music is therapeutic!
Cooking is therapeutic!
Art is therapeutic!
Sleep is therapeutic!
Shopping is therapeutic!

Reflection Notes: _____

_____

_____

_____

_____

_____

_____

_____

_____

_____

_____

_____

_____

_____

Chapter 7

The Accident

In February 2010, I was involved in a car accident that caused me to need spine surgery to correct my injury. A delivery truck rear-ended me causing my body to snap back and forward with the seat belt fastened tight. Anxiety rushed to my mind, and as I sat in pain and shock waiting for the ambulance to come, I heard these words, "I preserved you, I protected you, and I'm preparing you!" My mind began to recall the day's events up to that point. The first assignment for the day was a home-going service for a young man who was murdered. What a moving service where the presence of The Lord was evident and needed, especially during a time of sorrow. There I was, reflecting, and gratitude came over me as I realized that my family could have been preparing for my own home-going service in a flash; without warning it could have been me. There are events in life that can alter the very course you're on. There I was, traveling the world, empowering masses, physically capable of managing daily activities, agile, creative, young, and vibrant, and *now* here I am, starting physical therapy in order to help my body respond properly. I visited numerous specialists and lived with chronic pain daily. The norm I once knew became foreign to me.

By August of 2010 the surgeon performed disc fusion to C4 and C5 in my spine at *Franklin Hospital* in Long Island, NY. They cut the front of my neck in order to repair the part of my spine that was damaged. As a communicator through word and song, I couldn't help but wonder what the end result would be.

I chose to trust, and I resolved that whatever happened through the surgery, Gods "got me," so I would be good. It was a very serious surgery with no guarantees from anyone but God. I had a few visitors who came to see me . . . some I didn't expect to see and others I was hoping to see but didn't. Being hospitalized for five days, I needed the ministry of presence—something I learned about in chaplaincy classes. Sometimes you don't have to say anything; there's just something about showing up that makes all the difference in the world.

Everyone has a schedule but priorities speak very loud, and believe me, I heard loud and clear. The recovery process was even more painful than the surgery. When I awakened, my dad and stepmom were standing there looking at me as I came to, with a drain tube in my neck to prevent me from choking on my blood. The man who wasn't there throughout my life was now standing there with me, making sure I knew he was there. We've spent the last thirteen years growing in grace. Forgiveness, letting go, and reconciliation are crucial components in relationships.

Becoming better and not bitter will position you in a place of power. Even though I could barely talk, the communication was received. I'm a "Daddy's Girl." It always has been and will be that way, even with all the challenges. As I laid there unable to speak and move, something incredible happened inside of me. I saw a man trying to redeem the time during one of the hardest times of my life. Although my body was fragile, my spirit leaped and my soul was healing. The road to recovery was long, hard, and sometimes lonely. I lost a few friends along the way, met some new ones, and discovered the power of a good support system.

On Dec 17, 2010, I was preparing to reconnect with my intercessory prayer sisters at a fellowship, when I was moved to attend a service at Pilgrim Assemblies in Brooklyn instead. As much as I wanted to see my sisters, I knew where I needed to be. A young man I grew up with in the Baptist church was ministering that evening. He'd been elevated in ministry, which was certainly expected, even in his youth. He taught a word entitled, "Rebuke That Devil!" As he shared the word with power, I understood why it was imperative for me to be there. My feelings and my body were talking me out of participating in the fight from a clear perspective. "So then, faith comes by hearing, and hearing by the word of God" (Romans 10: 17 NKJV). I was in the fight of my life for my faith. After he taught and preached, we began to intercede together as a congregation. I guess I didn't miss intercessory prayer after all. While praying, he began laying hands on people and prophesying. As I was sitting there, I got the feeling that there was a specific word just for me. The man of God pointed to me and began to speak things, confirming my assignment, what has happened, what's to come, and that I have two years to get prepared. Although our churches visited each other in our youth, we didn't have a personal relationship, so he couldn't have known specifics. I left with a sense of closure and responsibility to let it all go and get going. After a full year of physical therapy, I graduated! By then I was home continuing the exercises and with each day I was overcoming.

In August 2011, as New York prepared for Hurricane Irene, I noticed something strange happening in my body. My speech was slurring slightly, headaches were more intense, and all I wanted to do was sleep. Of course, I thought there's no time for any of this, I must help prepare my family for the storm outside. No one knew that I was experiencing an internal storm. I began preparing my travel bag with toiletries while preparing food for the family simultaneously. My daughter noticed some challenges I was having, as my body began to go limp while I was sitting. She lifted me up and asked if I wanted her to tell her dad. I didn't want to bother anyone; as I stated before, it wasn't the time for this! For five days I battled with this strange experience. On day five I decided to go to the hospital and get checked out, knowing I'd be admitted. With my weave fully installed (by yours truly), my bag packed, and a French mani and pedi (by yours truly), I headed out. And although it was a struggle and uncomfortable, I realized that my gifts pushed me for the greater good, even in my pain.

The triage nurse evaluated me and by this time my speech was very bad, and I could barely walk. I was rushed from triage to a bed in the emergency room where the doctors were baffled at the symptoms. After a series of tests, I was admitted and went upstairs to a room. While there, a pastor from a church I visited came to see me. As she was praying, a prophetic word was spoken regarding dreams and visions. I thought to myself, I don't want to dream here, I want to dream in the comfort of my home. Sure enough, I began to see that night; The Lord shared with me that I needed help fighting this one, and he sent help! After five days in the hospital, and three days with no response in my right leg, intercessors from churches I've ministered at and grew up in showed up and helped me fight. After tests, scans, doctors, and specialists, I was diagnosed with a brain disorder. What!? I was getting stronger . . . how could this be? What happened? What's happening? I'm not even forty! The doctors released me to go home with home care because my insurance wouldn't cover rehab. Home care included three nurse visits and twelve hours of home attendant care . . . not per month or week, but that was it, in *total*! Thank God for my immediate family and friends who stepped in to help from time to time, and for my determination to fight and win!

Now I was back in physical therapy and after a year, I graduated again. By 2012, the doctor wrote me up as "totally disabled." Totally disabled . . . what does that mean? No work, fighting for social security disability, bills piling up, and having to choose whether I go to the doctor or use the co-pay to buy food or our necessities. This is not the way I imagined life would be. My husband and son stood together to do their best with what they had. Thank God for our anonymous angels who sowed, supported, and showed love during one of the hardest times in our lives. I realized that bad things happen to good people, and that by the grace of God they will pass, and growth *will* come out of it all—but only if you choose to grow.

In January 2012, I decided to sing once a month, out of obedience to the call on my life. Each time, I had the responsibility to push past the pain and discomfort, and pour out of my life to encourage others. It's amazing how I found strength by encouraging others, when I needed it myself. All the while I was overcoming silent fears, depression, discomfort, and uncertainty with a smile. There's a song I love to sing by recording artist and dear friend Darwin Hobbs entitled, "Champion!" Every word speaks of who I am and what I've been through, and when I sing it or hear it I can't help but get excited about where I am and where I'm going. After a full year, I found myself strengthened and encouraged to set new, realistic goals. I set a goal to walk over The Brooklyn Bridge in honor of anyone facing physical challenges. I called it "Walking with a Purpose." Experiencing the stigmas placed on people with any type of disability became my new reality. I now had a walker, three canes, an unpredictable body, a brain disorder with no natural cure, and dreams lying dormant—awaiting the opportunity to manifest.

In December 2012, I became a New York State Certified Chaplain through a ten-week training program for providing soul care for humanity. With my cane in tow, limp, and a desire to be better; I finished strong! Letting go of dead weight, relationships, and negative, paralyzing memories are critical to living in the present while setting and reaching goals. What you believe and how you see things will determine the choices you make. Renew your mind, develop your skills, manage expectations, and see obstacles as opportunities, not road blocks. Get the better of your struggle, then pay it forward by helping others. There's more than one way to experience relief from stress. Find positive ways to grow through and enjoy life.

In May 2013, my dad and I were on our way to his church, *Greater Allen Cathedral*, to celebrate his 65th birthday, something we had never done before, and we were in an accident. A truck t-boned us in the intersection while traveling through a green traffic light. Upon impact, we were injured. This accident sent me back to physical therapy for another six months. This time, the recovery process was less grueling and more progressive. There was no time to focus on the pain. My vantage point had changed; I was proactive and determined to defy the odds. After all, I was still labeled as "totally disabled." Thankfully, we're still here to tell about it.

The past few years have truly been a roller coaster ride filled with ups, downs, and unpredictable challenges. Nevertheless, I'm making some sweet lemonade. I believe this season of accidents saved my life. This involuntary sabbatical forced me to deal with and uproot some things that were hard to address. One by one, I believe that I've overcome the silent dream killers. On July 27, 2013 I decided to accomplish my goal of walking over the bridge with the support of dear friends. With my cane in hand and my knee brace on tight, we did it!

God is still sending help and I'm still fighting! Dad and I both had knee surgery in Aug 2013 and although this is a part of my story, I won't complain. The past four years has been tedious. I'm grieving the loss of three dear family members in three weeks, dear friends lost their mothers weeks apart, and I almost lost my mom twice this year. Some days are harder than others, but choosing to be free from any negative entanglements will keep you in a place of productivity. There's a book entitled *The Wounded Healer* by Henri J.M. Nouwen; and I believe we are all in many ways, just that. Although we may be wounded, we have the capacity to help heal others. It's possible to produce during imperfect conditions. Some of the greatest men and women experienced adversity but didn't succumb to the pressure or pain, and are very successful. I've heard it said that failure is the womb for success. Fear of failing will keep you from trying. Hurt people will continue the cycle, so choose the healing process in order to break the cycles. Here I am, living proof that in this life, things will happen within your control and without your permission. Regardless of what happens, choose life.

Reflection

Today is a great day to say, "YES!"

Yes to productivity!
Yes to rest!
Yes to balance!
Yes to creativity!
Yes to finishing strong!
Yes to adaptability!
Yes to developing your dream!
Yes to managing your time!
Yes to family!
Yes to constructive assessment!
Yes To healthy boundaries
Yes to the right relationships!

What would you say "YES" to?

Reflection Notes: _____

_____

_____

_____

_____

_____

_____

_____

_____

Chapter 8

Overcomer

Overcome:
to get the better of in a struggle or conflict; conquer, defeat.

What God says will surely come to pass! His methods may not make sense but His credit is good! Regardless of the facts, my truth is I win! How do you win with odds stacked against you? I'm glad you asked. You win by choosing to take control of your life, by making decisions based on truth and not your feelings, and by doing everything in your power to reach your goals. Be open to the right relationships and you will position yourself above the struggle, not in it. Procrastination and excuses are your enemy from within, not an enemy without. Life is filled with amazing opportunities, leading each individual down a path predestined for them. Hidden treasures are built within each earthen vessel, created for a specific purpose, discovered throughout the journey. Although we are not afforded the grace to choose the families were born into, we have a choice in how we relate to the culture as well as the possible challenges. If you want to see different fruit, it begins with planting good seeds. Some experiences in life will challenge you to detach from people. As a girl, I experienced a traumatic situation that altered my perspective on family, safety, trust, and forgiveness. My behavior reflected defense mechanisms in the most awkward situations. I realized some important things about myself: I not only resented the offender but also those I believed should have helped me; I found it hard to forgive myself even though I wasn't at fault; and I didn't want to hurt but I didn't know how to "let it go"!

I decided to take myself on a journey in order to filter my feelings and thoughts, and provide myself an opportunity for true healing. This process would require total honesty with myself and others, as well as cooperation. Only then would I experience freedom to accept soul care as needed. Hebrews 6:13 (*KJV*) reminds us, "Having done all, to stand." Both literally and figuratively, I choose to stand for what's right not just for who's right. I choose to stand firm and not be moved by what I've seen and continue to see. If decisions are rooted in one's character, I'll no longer excuse the inexcusable and accept the things I cannot change, but rather I will change the things I can no longer accept. I've learned that within every obstacle is an opportunity for growth.

We've heard it said that today's dung is tomorrow's fertilizer. The smart farmer processes the dung and uses it as fertilizer for future harvest. No matter what your past looks like there's potential in both the negative and the positive. So many people throw relationships away because of the work it takes to maintain them. Know the difference between unfruitful relationships and growing pains. Sometimes, in your toughest season, you can become a repellent and not even know it. Isolate *the problem*, not just yourself.

Grow through . . .
Forgive yourself and others,
Don't be afraid to ask for help,
Commit to the process of change.

The prisons of the mind are unhealthy places . . . deadly and unfruitful. They quietly rob you of a productive life filled with happiness, and a continual flow of healthy relationships. The mind's prisons are where many dreams are cut off, ceilings are lowered, limitations are fortified, confusion is glorified, and cycles of dysfunction are produced. These prisons may be qualified by negative words and experiences. Transformation truly takes place when positive information displaces the negative. What you think about will be reflected in your decisions, relationships, and self talk. Thoughts are opportunities. Whichever thought becomes a meditation, produces fruit, so choose your focused thoughts wisely. No one can hinder your progress or process except you!

Know your strengths and weaknesses (and vice versa).

Some women are better mothers than wives.
Some men are better fathers than husbands.
Some people are better teachers than students.
Some people are better listeners than speakers.
Some people light up a room just by entering.
Some people can clear out a room by entering.
Some people are thorough in some things and lazy in others.
Some people are bold in some things and fearful in others.

No matter where you are . . . choose to be your best you!

According to Romans 8:28, all things work together for my good. By faith, I stand on the promises of God with great expectations, trusting in His Sovereignty. As a strong woman, I've faced many challenges with support, and often alone. I found that people who present one face in public and another in private offered me fruitless experiences in relationships because of disagreement, discord, and disrespect. It's amazing how many people want you to you submit to polluted, dysfunctional environments and systems, and avoid confronting corrupt roots; yet with their mismanaged expectations, they expect healthy fruit. A tree will only bear fruit of its kind!

What do you meditate on often? Is it positive or negative? Think on good things, pure things, things of virtue, and things of good report! Whatever consumes your mind has control over your life. Thinking is free, context in thinking costs!

Are you replaying thoughts that produce strong negative feelings? Choose your daily meditation. Challenge yourself to *grow* through, not just *go* through. Decide to evict negativity out of your mind . . . it only occupies the space you give it.

God uses people as an answer to your need. Character check: if you have to manipulate people, abuse relationships or power, and use people to get what you want or need, then you deserve all the negativity those seeds produce. Don't pray for a crop failure . . . do right because it's right! It doesn't matter who you are, the office you hold, the position you're in, or the influence you have, God knows. He sees, and frustrating His grace is not a good look! If a man or woman has to use manipulation in order to get results, they may very well be uncovered for who they really are. God will certainly deal with such conduct, to lead that a person towards repentance and reconciliation.

"Work at getting along with each other and with God. Otherwise you'll never get so much as a glimpse of God. Make sure no one gets left out of God's generosity. Keep a sharp eye out for weeds of bitter discontent. A thistle or two gone to seed can ruin a whole garden in no time. Watch out for the Esau syndrome: trading away God's lifelong gift in order to satisfy a short-term appetite. You well know how Esau later regretted that impulsive act and wanted God's blessing—but by then it was too late, tears or no tears" (Hebrews 12:14-17 *MSG*).

The root of bitterness runs deep, infecting the entire being. What can cause a bitter root to grow?

Betrayal
Abandonment
Abuse (all types)
Disappointment

How can we uproot the negative, learn the lesson, and not become what hurt us?

Acknowledge it.
Assess it.
Accept the things you can't change.
Address the things you can change.

Some look for love from those who reject them. Some accept affection even when it's perverted. Until you accept the truth about God and His love for you (John 3:16), you'll repeat cycles, live beneath your privilege, and become a common waste place. Love God, self, and others.

You'll never know your capacity if you're not stretched. After stretching, you do not return to your past state mentally, emotionally, physically, and socially. Become better, not bitter; and wiser, not weaker, during growing seasons. Prayer changes things. Praising God changes your perspective and worship tenders the heart. Ecclesiastes 3:1 (*NKJV*) tells us, "To everything there is a season, and a time for every purpose under heaven."

. . . that moment when you accept the fact that it's past time to move! There are so many working definitions for the word "move." Within the pages of this book, you read about a few things that stood out to me. Your perspective will determine if the process and outcome will be positive or negative. I believe that this season is requiring one or more movements in order to experience the benefit of necessary modifications.

MOVE!

Move on,
Move out,
Move over,
Move up.

Assess Yourself,
Assist Yourself,
Assert Yourself.

Selah.

Woke up this morning in my feelings . . .

I feel like singing . . .
So I'll just go ahead and sing . . .
I feel like dancing . . .
So I'll just dance until I can't . . .
I feel like playing . . .
So I'll just live and laugh . . .
I feel like eating my favorite foods,
Going to my favorite places,
And enjoying the company of amazing people . . .
So I'll just do what I feel.

Reflection

Have you ever needed to have "real talk," and as you go through your list of people to talk to, you realize it's just as expensive for you to hold it in than to talk it out?

Reflection Notes: _____

_____

_____

_____

_____

_____

_____

_____

_____

_____

_____

_____

_____

_____

From Their Heart

Red (Husband):

A day full of sunshine quickly turned into an overcast. From an overcast, it turned into a rainstorm. A rainstorm turned into a spontaneous combustion. Everything exploded from inside out. I had a wife who worshipped and praised The Lord so boldly, proudly, and loudly. And then the record stopped (screech). My dove was now speechless. Motionless. She went from being a spry adult, to exhibiting the growth patterns of a toddler. She couldn't talk or walk. I was hurt, very hurt. I felt her strife in two fold, but I kept a straight face because I knew it would all be over within due time. Spiritual warfare reared its ugly head with many peaks and valleys. Her physical rehabilitation was the least of my worries; I took aim at her emotional and spiritual growth, along with her toughness to overcome this setback for the set up. Finding the balance of tough love and nurturing her was a task that I fell short of quite a few times. Her ails became my life, her pain is still embedded in my heart until this day. Why? Because I am her and she is me, we are one. However, I silently screamed for help. What about me? Who's helping me the midst of putting on a brave face for her sake? He told me to give it ALL to Him. I did. My God. And that's why we rejoice today. Shalom.

Davon Jay Redmond:

We can't make an announcement telling people with mental illnesses to speak up until we're ready for what they have to say, 'cause truth be told, the problem is that people don't receive it as something real, and people automatically assume you're lying or you're crazy. So we have to make sure we know of people and places that can help . . . places that won't just throw them on medication.

D'Asia Quane Redmond:

No matter WHAT was going on, my mom always made our house a home, from the food, the music we listened to, and our waking up to getting ready for school, to the Friday night prayer dinners she had with her friends and my siblings. I often stayed in her room and watched TV to the scent of the house after she cleaned it and lit candles. She always celebrated my siblings and me, allowing us to be ourselves even when she was down and out. She never missed a beat. Love you mommy.

Dhane Shaddai Redmond:

I am just so happy to be the daughter of a true warrior and conqueror. A few days ago my mommy performed in a showcase called *The Circles of Sisters*. It may not be a big deal to others but every time she goes on stage it gives me great joy. What was so special about this time was that she wore heels and she hasn't done so since the first accident—about three years ago. At home she would try them on for fun, and in the back of my mind I was screaming, "Mommy, take them off before I throw them out!" because it would scare me. So I put heels on to take her attention away from *her* wearing heels to *me* wearing heels. Unfortunately, I had to wear a couple before she actually sat down. God knows I hate heels, but I love my mommy and her safety more than I hate heels. Long story short, mommy, I am so proud of you, and I love you.

Dallas Shalom Redmond:

When mommy had her accident, I was turning three years old in three months. She couldn't play with me like she used to because of pain. I would pick flowers for her on my way home from *Sunshine Day Care* to make her feel better. I prayed for her to get better, helped in any way I could, and tried to make her happy. I'm so thankful she's stronger today! My mommy is truly an overcomer!

My Dear Friend/Sis Sabrina Lamour:

I've personally witnessed Malissa's journey of overcoming every obstacle in her life but I don't think anything could have prepared me for witnessing her biggest battle yet.

Looking back, I can see how every obstacle she overcame prior to the accident, was strengthening and preparing her for what would be years of physical, mental, emotional, and to some degree, spiritual pain and development.

I'll never forget the day I learned of her accident. Betwixt and between the memories and hopes were fears that my friend may never walk or talk again. Questions like, "What about her ministry?" and "What about her worship through song?" and "What about her voice?" and "What about her promises?" flooded my mind and heart, but little did I know that God was going to prove to not only me, but the world what Malissa was really made of.

One day I picked her up. It was my first time seeing her walk with a cane. I wanted to be sad. I wanted to be angry. But I couldn't. I didn't understand why of all people, her. Those feelings quickly became overshadowed by the laughter, tears, and transparency that have always been.

They say serving The Lord does not mean you won't face tough times because it's through challenges that our faith and character are developed. I can't imagine someone who has demonstrated more tenacity, courage, determination, and strength than Malissa, especially over the last five plus years.

Her joy was and continues to be unmatched. Her faith was and continues to be unshakable and unwavering. She believed God would pull her through, and pull her through He did.

From Malissa to Her Husband, Red:

I send special love to my husband for helping me to get through a tough season of ministry. I know it's not easy for you to witness my journey and I truly appreciate your heart and growth. It's great to know that no matter what happens outside, you pay attention and you look for ways to minister to me, and for that I'm grateful.

Appendix 1

The National Suicide Prevention Lifeline is a national network of local crisis centers that provides free and confidential emotional support—twenty four hours a day and seven days a week—to people who are in suicidal crisis or in emotional distress. They are committed to continually improving crisis services and advancing suicide prevention by empowering individuals, advancing professional best practices, and building awareness.

"We can all help prevent suicide. The Lifeline provides 24/7, free and confidential support for people in distress, prevention and crisis resources for you or your loved ones, and best practices for professionals."

Source: *The National Suicide Prevention Lifeline* website, SuicidePreventionLifeline.org

1-800-273-8255

Appendix 2

Depression

Depression takes on many different faces; it's the silent dream killer.

"Depression (major depressive disorder or clinical depression) is a common but serious mood disorder. It causes severe symptoms that affect how you feel, think, and handle daily activities, such as sleeping, eating, or working. To be diagnosed with depression, the symptoms must be present for at least two weeks."

Source: *The National Institute of Mental Health* website, nimh.nih.gov

Post-Traumatic Stress Disorder

"PTSD is a disorder that develops in some people who have experienced a shocking, scary, or dangerous event. It is natural to feel afraid during and after a traumatic situation. Fear triggers many split-second changes in the body to help defend against danger or to avoid it. This "fight-or-flight" response is a typical reaction meant to protect a person from harm. Nearly everyone will experience a range of reactions after trauma, yet most people recover from initial symptoms naturally. Those who continue to experience problems may be diagnosed with

PTSD. People who have PTSD may feel stressed or frightened even when they are not in danger."

Source: *The National Institute of Mental Health* website, nimh.nih.gov

ForSmiles Inc.
Consulting Services

To contact the author, Malissa Redmond,
please use the email address below:

ForSmiles4@gmail.com

About Malissa Redmond

Malissa Redmond is a Brooklyn native who grew up in the Baptist church, where she began singing in the choir at a young age. She served in *Rugged Cross Baptist Church* faithfully in the music department as Choir Director, Sunbeam Supervisor, lead soloist, and wherever needed until The Lord transitioned her to *Christian Cultural Center* under the leadership of Dr. A.R. Bernard Sr. and Elder Karen Bernard. The anointing to sing introduced her to the call to preach and teach. It elevated her to the ministerial staff where Pastor and Elder mentor her personally.

Malissa has traveled the world ministering the gospel in Italy, England, Australia, the Bahamas, Austria, Aruba, Trinidad, Tobago, and has appeared on many stages across the United States. Malissa is also a New York State Certified Chaplain. It is her desire to fulfill the plan of God on her life, edifying the kingdom, sharing the good news, and serving humanity.

Malissa Redmond is the president and CEO of one of the newest consulting services in the industry, *ForSmiles Inc.* As a Certified Event and Hospitality Manager, with an impassioned love for people and providing quality service, the Brooklyn native plans to bring a special personal touch to the beneficiaries of her company. As a former director of administration and sixteen years as an arts consultant, she brings her knowledge and expertise on connecting the dots and helping her clients reach their goals, one project at a time. In addition to launching her family owned and operated business in 2014, she's had the pleasure of using her gifts in the arts to travel the world and work with some outstanding people in both the gospel and secular industries. Malissa is currently the Executive Consultant for *The Phil Taitt Show*. She and her team worked tirelessly for *Dream/Reach/Inspire* 2016 to make it a huge success. They provided private security, elite car service, event and hospitality management, and makeup and production support. Looking forward, the future is blessed and bright for *ForSmiles Inc*. Many have already been touched by Malissa's God-given abilities through venues like *Trinity Broadcast Network*, *The Today Show*, *Bobby Jones Gospel*, *Carnegie Hall*, and *Gospel Super Fest*. Be on the lookout . . . great things are in store.

Live On Purpose, With Purpose!

Splendor Publishing

Splendor Publishing's life-changing books are written by skilled and passionate leaders, entrepreneurs, and experts with a mission to make a positive impact in the lives of others.

Splendor books inspire and encourage personal, professional, and spiritual growth. For information about our book titles, authors, or publishing process, or for wholesale ordering for conferences, seminars, events, or training, visit SplendorPublishing.com.

CPSIA information can be obtained
at www.ICGtesting.com
Printed in the USA
BVHW041553221219
567504BV00014B/2359/P